D1066577

GOT PROMOTED? GET PROMOTED. (AGAIN)

VOLUME 01: YOUR FIRST 100 DAYS
ACCELERATE LEADERSHIP PERFORMANCE IN YOUR FIRST 100 DAYS

BY NIAMH O'KEEFFE
FOUNDER & MANAGING DIRECTOR OF FIRST100™

Published and distributed by
First100™ Ltd 2009
The Coach House,
16a Nottingham Street,
London, W1U 5NF
www.first100.co.uk

A CIP catalogue record for this book is
available from the British Library.

ISBN: 978-0-9564118-0-8

Printed in the United Kingdom by
Gyroscope Ltd, Manchester.

With our special thanks to Simon Andrews
and Matthew Winward for their role in
bringing this book to life. And special
thanks to Garrett O'Keeffe and Eimee
Kuah for their important role as members
of the First100™ Leadership Team.

CONTENTS

YOUR FIRST 100 DAYS JOURNEY

INTRODUCTION

FOREWORD:
FIRST100™ FOUNDER & MANAGING DIRECTOR, NIAMH O'KEEFFE

INSIGHT ON 'FIRST 100 DAYS'

Through my experience as a headhunter placing senior executives in the City of London, I realised that the first 100 Days was the most crucial stage in the lifecycle of a new leadership appointment. My observation was that failure to optimise the first 100 days was probably the biggest missed trick on leadership effectiveness and performance acceleration.

FIRST100™ COMPANY

My prior background of 8 years as a strategy and management consultant at Accenture meant I was well equipped to convert this insight into a new niche 'first 100 days' consultancy offering. I founded First100™ in 2004. Since then, my team and I have worked alongside senior executives of global organisations, as leadership coaches and trusted companions during their first 100 day journeys.

OUR CLIENTS CONSISTENTLY OFFER A SMALL BUT GOOD WORD – "USEFUL" – TO DESCRIBE FIRST100™ ADVICE. MY INTENTION FOR THIS BOOK IS THAT IT HAS THE SAME EFFECT.

USE

FOREWORD:
FIRST100™ GLOBAL MARKETING DIRECTOR, FIONA O'KEEFFE

PRACTICAL INSIGHTS

A perceptive book, grounded in practical reality, for senior executives who want to achieve accelerated success in the first 100 days of a leadership appointment. The first 100 days is a pressurised moment of need, and intellectualisation of the issues is hardly helpful. What Niamh offers is practical guidance, thoughtful insights and useful advice that is immediately implementable.

SPEED–READ

In keeping with the theme of 'acceleration', Niamh has organised this book in a 'speed-read' style for the time-pressured leader. Deliberately concise, this book provides the crucial insights to empower you to achieve greatest success during this intense early phase.

OUR FIRST100™ CLIENT TRACK RECORD INCLUDES WORKING WITH SENIOR EXECUTIVES FROM TELECOMMUNICATIONS (EG. BT, EIRCOM, O2, VODAFONE), PHARMACEUTICALS (EG. BOSTON SCIENTIFIC, GENZYME, TEVA, MCKESSON), TECHNOLOGY COMPANIES (EG. ACCENTURE, MC AFEE) AND OTHERS, INCLUDING ENERGY COMPANIES (EG. BP) AND FMCG (EG. JOHN WEST).

FUL

NOTE TO READER

You are an important person, because you are
a leader with responsibility for others. I see you as
a whole person: an emotional being as well as a
business brain and a talented being. I see you as
a learner, open to guidance and advice because
you are stepping up to a role that you have never
done before.

IT IS MAKE OR BREAK TIME.

In the first 100 days, even more so than any other time in the lifecycle of a leadership appointment, all eyes are on you. It is a time of pressure, of scrutiny. It is make or break time as to whether you lay down the right foundation for the rest of your first year and beyond.

I want to help you achieve success in your first 100 days, so that everybody benefits: you, your team, the organisation who hired or promoted you, and all your role stakeholders.

I have stepped back from my day to day role, as First100™ Coach, and attempted to gather my specialist first 100 days knowledge and experience into a book that is useful to you.

Please enjoy reading this book. I hope you find it both strategic and pragmatic in its approach, with some good ideas and insights, grounded in the commercial reality of your situation.

WISHING YOU WELL ON YOUR FIRST 100 DAYS JOURNEY.

NIAMH O'KEEFFE

THE IMPORTANCE OF THE
FIRST 100 DAYS

SHRINKING TIME PRESSURES

Performance acceleration is a critical business demand in today's global economy. A few decades ago investors sought 10 year strategic plans, then 5 year and subsequently 3 year plans were in vogue. Since 2007, I noticed the emergence of the 'Two Year Plan' from forward-thinking CEOs and business leaders.

Now, more than ever, the pressure is on to recover high return on investments, so companies and shareholders need their leaders to perform better and faster than ever before.

In this ever-shrinking time pressure context, the first 100 days of a new leadership role appointment becomes increasingly important.

FOR CHIEF EXECUTIVES OF COMPANIES LISTED ON THE STOCK MARKET, THE FIRST 100 DAYS IS THE APPROXIMATE TIME BETWEEN THE DAY THEY START A NEW JOB AND WALL STREET'S APPRAISAL OF THEIR PERFORMANCE.

TIME IS UP FOR THE FIRST THREE MONTHS TO BE SEEN AS THE 'SETTLING IN' PERIOD.

10, 5, 3, 2 YEAR STRATEGIC PLAN.

THE IMPORTANCE OF THE FIRST 100 DAYS

MANY STAKEHOLDERS AND THE STAKES ARE HIGH

The hiring manager, incumbent team and other role stakeholders in the organisation typically view a new leadership appointment with a mixture of both relief and apprehension.

Senior appointments are not made lightly – typically the stakes are high, a significant change is necessary and people are looking to the new leader for answers and a clear pathway forward.

The first phase of a new leadership appointment not only represents a fresh starting point, but also raises concerns about how to make it work. It is a time of mutual scrutiny, and a successful first 100 days has a major determining impact on success within the first 12 months and beyond.

YOUR CAREER MAY DEPEND ON IT

Notwithstanding the responsibility on the leader to consider the impact on the team and organisation at large, the talented senior executive is also self-motivated to accelerate performance in the first 100 days in order to enjoy an accelerated career.

JUDGEMENTS ON A FAST TRACK LEADER'S SUCCESS IN THE FIRST 100 DAYS OF A NEW ROLE CAN BE QUICKLY FOLLOWED BY JUDGEMENTS ABOUT HIS OR HER LEADERSHIP POTENTIAL FOR SUCCESS IN THE NEXT STEP UP ROLE IN 2-3 YEARS TIME.

GET IT RIGHT FROM THE BEGINNING AND EVERYBODY BENEFITS.

EXECUTIVE SUMMARY

I. BEGINNING

WILL I SUCCEED OR FAIL?

Role 'beginnings' bring a heady mix of excitement, anticipation and nervousness too. There is a feeling of being the 'special one' – singled out from others to take on an important role.

HOWEVER, THERE IS ALSO A FEELING OF TREPIDATION – AM I REALLY GOOD ENOUGH? WILL I SUCCEED OR FAIL?

Leaders, however experienced, are emotional beings just like everybody else. In my experience everybody who is facing into their first 100 days oscillates between these feelings of 'special one'/ superiority and 'worried one'/inferiority. Regulating your emotions during the beginning stage of your first 100 days is an important key to your success. Neither be over-confident, nor blinded by panic and fear of failure. Stay centred, stay grounded, stay calm and confident, and you will be just fine.

CHAPTER 01: PREPARE
LET GO OF YOUR PREVIOUS ROLE

Saying your first step is to hand over your current role may seem like stating the obvious, but in my experience people do not detach fast enough.

Letting go of current attachments as quickly as possible is a crucial first step because you need to refocus all your time, energy and thoughts on the new role. So remember, however committed a person you are - your last role was your responsibility, but it is not your responsibility anymore. As soon as you hand in your notice, start to close out the previous role immediately.

IT IS OVER, SO HAND IT OVER.

In my experience some senior executives stay involved in their previous role for all the wrong reasons eg. preference to stay in comfort zone, concern about managing their legacy, emotional ties to team, false belief that no one else could be good enough to take over.

I ALWAYS CHECK THAT MY CLIENTS ARE 100% DETACHED FROM OLD ROLES AND 100% FOCUSSED ON THE NEW ROLE, OTHERWISE WE ARE OFF TO A SLOW START.

If you're an internal appointee, letting go can be understandably harder than for an external hire that contractually leaves the company and physically leaves a building.

Your transition may also be tougher if you are expected to do both roles until your successor is found. Add to this the fact that as an internal appointee, you are already a known entity, 'institutionalised' and most likely 'pre-programmed' on the issues. It's tough to bring a fresh perspective if you have always been there.

Let's face it; an external appointee with none of the internal baggage may have an initial advantage by simply turning up.

SO WHAT CAN AN INTERNAL APPOINTEE DO TO GET OFF TO AN ACCELERATED START IN THE FIRST 100 DAYS?

BE VERY ASSERTIVE AND ARTIFICIALLY RECREATE THE SAME CONTEXT OF AN EXTERNAL HIRE.

Accelerating success in your first 100 days is already compromised if you are attempting to overlap 2 jobs at once, so:

– NEGOTIATE A CLEAR FINISHING DATE FOR CURRENT ROLE.

– APPOINT AN 'INTERIM' IF YOUR SUCCESSOR IS NOT IN SITU AND FULLY HANDOVER.

– AGREE A FORMAL STARTING DATE OF NEW ROLE, AND DON'T START UNTIL THEN.

REST, RECOVER & READY YOURSELF.

The first 100 days is an intense phase – all eyes are on you and there is considerable pressure to perform and deliver early. So, in preparation, create time in-between roles to rest, recover from previous role and get ready for the new challenge ahead.

Think of yourself as a corporate athlete resting between serious races.

My suggestion to clients is to take a minimum of a fortnight full-time holiday break in between roles. This will clear your head from the old role and heighten energy levels and perspective coming into the first 100 days of the new role. You need to be fit for purpose, with a surplus of energy to take on a new role and make a strong early impact.

ENERGY MANAGEMENT IN THE FIRST 100 DAYS

TAKE CARE OF YOUR MIND.	BEFORE, DURING AND AFTER WORK: SCHEDULE ENOUGH TIME AND SPACE TO BE ON YOUR OWN TO RELAX AND RELEASE THE BUILD UP OF PRESSURE.
TAKE CARE OF YOUR BODY.	EXERCISE ROUTINELY, EAT HEALTHY AND NUTRITIOUS FOOD. TRY TO BUILD UP EXTRA RESERVE IN YOUR SYSTEM
ENLIST OTHERS TO SUPPORT YOU.	HIRE A FIRST100™ COACH. MAINTAIN A CALM AND NURTURING PERSONAL LIFE. NEGOTIATE EXTRA SUPPORT AND LATITUDE FROM LOVED ONES.

CHAPTER 01: PREPARE

Don't think this next 100 days is business as usual in your personal life. Starting a new role is a heightened stress event. Adrenalin will compensate for any lack of reserves, but don't exacerbate the pressure on you by having the house re-decorated or the in-laws coming for a visit (!).

KEEP A COOL, CLEAR HEAD AND MAINTAIN A CALM PERSONAL LIFE IF YOU WANT TO ENJOY ACCELERATED SUCCESS IN THE FIRST 100 DAYS.

Earlier in my coaching career I noticed a pattern of leaders feeling poorly during their first 100 days. It typically presented itself as my clients telling me, in passing, that they have a 'major cold'. And it was always accompanied with an air of surprise:

'I'M NEVER USUALLY ILL.'

It was being mentioned as if it was a completely separate event and not linked to the context of the heightened stress from the new job – demonstrating a total lack of awareness of the cause (major stress) and effect (major cold).

Now I proactively educate my clients to acknowledge that what is going on in their bodies can represent a physical manifestation or fallout from the challenge of the first 100 days. We get ahead of the curve, by adopting tactics to manage or mitigate rising stress levels early.

CHAPTER 01: PREPARE
UNDERSTAND TRANSITION 'GIVENS'

The primary task for the executive targeting first 100 days success is to set out the right strategic priorities, and stay focussed on them.

SOUNDS SIMPLE?

Unfortunately it is easier said than done. In my experience, there is a list of common challenges inherent in every transition that will affect the newly appointed executive. These can derail good intentions and get in the way of successfully achieving that primary task.

Each one is worthy of consideration, so read through the list and take some time to reflect on how each of these transition risks applies to your context.

TRANSITION 'GIVENS' FACING SENIOR EXECUTIVES IN THE FIRST 100 DAYS.

- TIME PRESSURES & INTENSE LEARNING CURVE.

- BEING OVER-WHELMED WITH IMMEDIATE 'FIRE-FIGHTING' AND TASK-DRIVEN PRIORITIES.

- NEED TO INVEST IN BUILDING NEW NETWORKS AND FORGE NEW STAKEHOLDER RELATIONSHIPS.

- DEALING WITH LEGACY ISSUES FROM THE PREDECESSOR.

- CHALLENGES ON INHERITING OR BUILDING A TEAM AND HAVING TO MAKE TOUGH PERSONNEL DECISIONS.

- FOR EXTERNAL HIRES, A LACK OF EXPERIENCE OF NEW COMPANY CULTURE MAY LEAD TO INADVERTENT GAFFES AND EARLY POLITICAL BLUNDERS – ALL OF WHICH CAN TAKE TIME TO RECOVER.

- GETTING THE BALANCE RIGHT BETWEEN MOVING TOO FAST AND MOVING TOO SLOWLY.

CHAPTER 01: PREPARE

TRANSITION 'GIVENS'	DESCRIPTIONS
TIME PRESSURES & INTENSE LEARNING CURVE.	IT TAKES TIME TO GET UP TO SPEED ON THE CONTENT OF YOUR NEW POSITION, AND YET BUSINESS AND MARKETS CANNOT SLOW DOWN AND WAIT FOR YOU TO CATCH UP. DECISIONS STILL NEED TO BE TAKEN AND CONSEQUENTLY THE PRESSURE CAN BUILD UP AND WILL NEED TO BE MANAGED IN ORDER TO STAY OPERATING EFFECTIVELY.
BEING OVER-WHELMED WITH IMMEDIATE 'FIRE- FIGHTING' AND TASK-DRIVEN PRIORITIES.	IT WOULD BE TEMPTING TO 'GET BUSY' AND DIVE INTO THE IMMEDIATE BUSINESS TASKS AND ISSUES. BUT YOU NEED TO HAVE THE STRENGTH OF CHARACTER TO STEP BACK AND TAKE TIME OUT TO LOOK AT THE BIG PICTURE: WHAT TASKS SHOULD YOU CONTINUE, WHAT SHOULD YOU STOP, AND WHAT SHOULD YOU START.
NEED TO INVEST IN BUILDING NEW NETWORKS AND FORGE NEW STAKEHOLDER RELATIONSHIPS.	THERE IS NO POINT IN HAVING THE RIGHT VISION AND STRATEGY IN ISOLATION – BRING PEOPLE WITH YOU. THE CULTURE MAY BE DENSE AND SLOW MOVING – PEOPLE MAY BE RESISTANT TO THE CHANGES YOU BRING. INVEST EARLY IN THE INFLUENCER AND STAKEHOLDER NETWORK.
DEALING WITH LEGACY ISSUES FROM THE PREDECESSOR.	DEPENDING ON THE QUALITY OF YOUR PREDECESSOR, YOUR UNIT MAY OR MAY NOT HAVE A GOOD REPUTATION, AND YOUR TEAM MAY HAVE DEVELOPED POOR HABITS, BEHAVIOURS AND DISCIPLINES THAT WILL TAKE TIME TO ADDRESS. OR YOU MAY HAVE TO ENDURE THE SCENARIO OF FILLING THE SHOES OF A MUCH-LOVED PREDECESSOR AND BEING RESENTED AS THE NEW GUY WHOSE MANDATE IS TO CHANGE HOW THINGS HAVE ALWAYS BEEN DONE BEFORE.

TRANSITION 'GIVENS'	DESCRIPTIONS
CHALLENGES ON INHERITING OR BUILDING A TEAM AND HAVING TO MAKE TOUGH PERSONNEL DECISIONS.	DON'T EXPECT UNDER-PERFORMERS TO HAVE BEEN WEEDED OUT PRIOR TO YOUR ARRIVAL. A KEY TASK IN YOUR FIRST 100 DAYS WILL BE TO ASSESS THE QUALITY OF YOUR TEAM: WHO STAYS, WHO GOES, AND WHO ELSE IS NEEDED ONBOARD. AND UNFORTUNATELY, YOUR BEST PERFORMER IS PROBABLY NOW DE-MOTIVATED AND RESENTFUL – AND CONSEQUENTLY UNDER-PERFORMING - BECAUSE HE APPLIED UNSUCCESSFULLY FOR YOUR JOB.
FOR EXTERNAL HIRES, A LACK OF EXPERIENCE OF NEW COMPANY CULTURE MAY LEAD TO INADVERTENT GAFFES AND EARLY POLITICAL BLUNDERS – ALL OF WHICH CAN TAKE TIME TO RECOVER.	FROM THE INNOCUOUS TO THE SIGNIFICANT, EVERYTHING YOU DO IS BEING JUDGED AS INDICATIVE OF YOUR CHARACTER. MERELY CHECKING YOUR BLACKBERRY DURING A MEETING MAY DEEPLY OFFEND YOUR NEW ROLE STAKEHOLDERS WHO MAY JUDGE THAT ACTION AS AN INDICATION THAT YOU ARE BRASH, DISINTERESTED AND ARROGANT. YOU WILL NEED TO BE ON 'HYPER ALERT' TO CONSCIOUSLY PICK UP CLUES ON THE ACCEPTABLE NORMS AND BEHAVIOURS.
GETTING THE BALANCE RIGHT BETWEEN MOVING TOO FAST AND MOVING TOO SLOWLY.	NEW APPOINTEES SOMETIMES PANIC AND THIS CAN RESULT IN EITHER DOING TOO MUCH (SCATTER GUN APPROACH, BUT NOT TACKLING THE CORE ISSUES) OR DOING TOO LITTLE ('I'LL JUST LISTEN FOR THE FIRST 3 MONTHS, AND THEN DECIDE WHAT TO DO'). NEITHER EXTREME CUTS IT. FIND THE RIGHT BALANCE.

CHAPTER 01: PREPARE
BUILD PROFILE OF ROLE,
ORGANISATION AND MARKET

"WHOLE SYSTEM" APPROACH

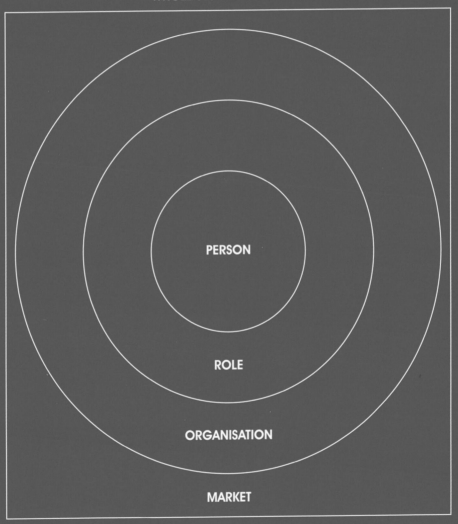

PERSON

ROLE

ORGANISATION

MARKET

STEP BACK AND TAKE A WIDE-LENS VIEW OF THE
'WHOLE SYSTEM' WITHIN WHICH YOU WILL BE
OPERATING. SEE IT IS AS A CONSTRUCT WHERE YOU
ARE AT THE CENTRE: THE PERSON (YOU, AS LEADER),
IN A ROLE, IN AN ORGANISATION, AND SET IN THE
CONTEXT OF YOUR MARKETPLACE/WORLD.

BUILD UP A PROFILE OF EACH COMPONENT IN
YOUR PARTICULAR SYSTEM, IN ORDER TO MAP
OUT THE LANDSCAPE OF YOUR OPPORTUNITIES
AND CHALLENGES.

PROFILING EXERCISE:

PROFILE THE PERSON:
(YOU, AS LEADER)

WHAT IS THE LEADERSHIP 'STEP UP' FOR YOU
(EG. PROMOTION TO MANAGING A FUNCTION
FOR THE FIRST TIME? A SWITCH FROM FUNCTIONAL
EXPERT TO GENERAL MANAGER? FROM MANAGING
A BUSINESS TO MANAGING AN ENTERPRISE?)

WHAT STRENGTHS, TOOLS, AND EXPERIENCES CAN
YOU UNIQUELY BRING TO THE ROLE THAT YOU CAN
LEVERAGE TO MAKE AN EARLY IMPACT, AND CAN
ACCELERATE EARLY PERFORMANCE?

CHAPTER 01: PREPARE

PROFILE THE ROLE:	IS THERE A LEARNING CURVE ON INDUSTRY, PRODUCT, STRATEGY THAT YOU CAN START TO TACKLE NOW, AHEAD OF STARTING?
	WHAT HAVE YOU BEEN ASKED TO DO? WHAT ARE THE EXPECTED ROLE DELIVERABLES?
	WHAT DO YOU KNOW ABOUT THE CAPABILITY OF YOUR TEAM? WHAT ARE THE GAPS?
	FIND OUT WHAT HAS BEEN COMMUNICATED TO OTHERS ABOUT YOU, AND YOUR MANDATE.
PROFILE THE ORGANISATION:	WHAT IS YOUR VISION FOR THE ROLE? HOW DOES YOUR VISION FOR THIS ROLE LINK TO THE VISION AND MISSION OF THE ORGANISATION? HOW CAN YOU CREATE VALUE FOR THE ORGANISATION?
	LOOK AT THE COMPANY WEBSITE TO PROFILE THE CEO AND TOP LEADERSHIP TEAM. WHO ARE YOUR ROLE STAKEHOLDERS? WHO ARE THE KEY DECISION-MAKERS, WHO ARE THE INFLUENCERS, WHO ARE THE POTENTIAL BLOCKERS?
	WHAT DO YOU KNOW ABOUT THE CULTURE OF THIS ORGANISATION, UNIT, TEAM – ITS NORMS AND VALUES?

PROFILE THE MARKET/ WORLD SYSTEM:

CONSIDER THE MARKET – WHO IS YOUR CUSTOMER (INTERNAL AND/OR EXTERNAL)? WHO ARE YOUR COMPETITORS? WHAT IS THE BIGGEST MARKET CHALLENGE FACING YOU IN THIS ROLE? WHAT ARE THE MARKET DYNAMICS? EG. GROWTH VS DECLINE.

Using these cues, take the time to think widely and deeply to build up the picture of what you are facing, so that you more quickly understand and navigate the whole system in the first 100 days.

Don't rush to judgement too early. You may have some information at this stage, but remember you have not met all the players yet, and you don't have experience of the actual role yet.

Be like a detective who has clues, but not yet all of the information pieced together.

Find the right balance of building up a profile of what is ahead and at the same time, reserve final judgement so that you can wisely allow reality and your own personal experience to adjust your perspective once you have started.

CHAPTER 01: PREPARE
GET READY TO WRITE YOUR
FIRST 100 DAYS PLAN

The first 100 days are characterised by an intense learning curve and overwhelm on the amount of tasks and issues to solve. In my experience, the biggest challenge facing newly appointed leaders is establishing the right set of strategic priorities, and then staying focussed on them.

SO, HOW DO YOU SET OUT THE RIGHT SET OF STRATEGIC PRIORITIES?

START WITH THE END IN MIND

A) ENVISAGE A TWO-YEAR ROLE HORIZON.

B) AGREE YOUR 12 MONTH BUSINESS PRIORITIES.

C) WRITE YOUR FIRST 100 DAYS PLAN.

CHAPTER 01: PREPARE

"IF YOU DON'T KNOW WHERE YOU ARE GOING, YOU WILL END UP IN THE WRONG PLACE…"

A) ENVISAGE A TWO-YEAR ROLE HORIZON

Even if your role contract is for 3 years or more or timelines unstated, my advice is that you assume you are leaving in 2 years. This gives you a sense of urgency in which to 'attack' the core role challenges. And if you take a view that you can do a 3 year role in 2 years, then you are more likely to be promoted into your next role faster!

With timelines shrinking even faster than ever before, it's more realistic for high performing leaders to have a 2 year role tenure, and either way it forces the pace. Seeing 3 years into the future is harder than ever. 2 years is just about possible. And anything less than 2 years would be short-termism and is not conducive to vision development and strategic planning.

AT THE END OF THE 2 YEARS IF YOU REMAIN CONTRACTED TO THAT ROLE FOR ANOTHER YEAR OR MORE, THEN SET OUT A NEW PLAN AT THAT STAGE, AND ACT LIKE IT IS A FRESH START IN ORDER TO REJUVENATE AND REFRESH YOUR APPROACH TO THE ROLE.

CHAPTER 01: PREPARE

Write a list of what you would like to have achieved with this role by the end of the 2 years encompassing:

– VISION & STRATEGY.

– PEOPLE & TEAMS.

– RESULTS & DELIVERABLES.

THERE IS A PROBLEMATIC DOWNSIDE AT TIMES IN THE CASE OF LEADERS WHO OPERATE WITH A 2 YEAR ROLE HORIZON, IF THEY ACCELERATE PACE BUT COMPROMISE LONG TERM STRATEGY AND INVESTMENTS.

My advice to executives is to remember that their role legacy will come back to haunt their long term career if they don't get it right, so don't focus on short term gains only, think about your role contribution in a stewardship fashion and how your lasting legacy and reputation in each role lives beyond the lifetime of your appointment.

B) AGREE YOUR FIRST 12 MONTH BUSINESS PRIORITIES

You will have picked up the key priorities and role requirements during the recruitment interviews or promotion process.

However, that phase may have including a 'selling' of the role to you – and some difficult challenges or priorities may have been mentioned but perhaps not in all their full glorious detail! In my experience, for external recruits, the selling process may even have involved taking out or 'softening' the reality of the true challenges of the role.

Also, if you had to give 3 or more months notice before starting, it is inevitable that priorities will have shifted and new external factors are in the mix by now.

So now is the time, when contracts have been signed or promotion agreed, and you are committed, to arrange another meeting with your hiring manager and other relevant stakeholders to agree on the first 12 month priorities.

CLEARLY THIS IS ALSO THE OPPORTUNITY TO SOLICIT INFORMATION FROM YOUR BOSS ON WHAT IS EXPECTED FROM YOU IN THE FIRST 100 DAYS.

CHAPTER 01: PREPARE

C) WRITE YOUR FIRST 100 DAYS PLAN
The First 100 Days Plan should set out what you want to have delivered by the end of the first 100 days. And it should be structured using monthly milestones (@30 days, @60 days, @90 days) to facilitate monthly reviews and keep your plan on track.

SOUNDS STRAIGHTFORWARD?

It should be. However, in my experience, executives don't write proper 100 day plans. Instead they write lists. They either have a set of themes or a list of things to do in their first 100 days, and they confuse this with having a plan. Plainly put, a set of key themes or a to-do list is not a First 100 Days Plan.

Also, surprisingly, executives tend to narrow their role rather than see it in its full expansive glory.

For example, executives tend to view their role as their individual functional area, rather than remember that they must also be a team member at peer level and deliver value in the wider sphere. Being a leader of the firm, faced with the overwhelm of a new role and new context, many executives oversimplify their plan by focussing on one key deliverable eg. the new Marketing Director focuses on delivering the Marketing Plan. And then subsequently they focus on the next task eg. building the team. This linear single-tasking approach makes for a very slow start.

IF YOU TRULY WANT TO ACCELERATE YOUR PERFORMANCE AND DELIVER MASSIVE EARLY SUCCESS IN A MANAGEABLE WAY, THEN READ ON AND I WILL EXPLAIN THE FIRST100 APPROACH TO TACKLING AND DEVELOPING AN OPTIMAL FIRST 100 DAYS PLAN.

PLAINLY PUT, A SET OF KEY THEMES OR A TO-DO LIST IS NOT A FIRST 100 DAYS PLAN.

CHAPTER 01: PREPARE
FIRST100ASSIST™: HOW TO WRITE YOUR FIRST 100 DAYS PLAN

FIRST100ASSIST™ FRAMEWORK: A "WHOLE SYSTEM" APPROACH

HOW TO WRITE YOUR FIRST 100 DAYS PLAN:

Since 2004, we have developed more than one hundred First 100 Days Plans. We have continuously improved our approach in response to our clients' needs. As such, we have amassed considerable experience and expertise on what constitutes a best practice First 100 Days Plan.

With that as context, I designed the First100assist™ framework whereby for the purposes of first 100 days, we take any leadership role and reframe it by splitting it across the whole system view and devising 10 key constituent roles.

FIRST100ASSIST™ FRAMEWORK
IN THE FIRST 100 DAYS OF YOUR LEADERSHIP ROLE,
WE BELIEVE YOU HAVE TO BE:

ON PERSON: A TRANSITION MAKER, A UNIQUE CONTRIBUTOR.

ON ROLE: A CONTENT LEARNER, A BUSINESS ACHIEVER,
A TEAM BUILDER, A COMMUNICATIONS PROVIDER.

ON ORGANISATION: A RELATIONSHIP BUILDER, A VALUE ADDER,
A CULTURE NAVIGATOR.

ON MARKET: A MARKET PLAYER.

I crafted 10 constituent roles because I reckoned that 10 was wide-reaching enough – any less is not stretching enough, and any more than 10 would be unwieldy.

STEP 1:
START WITH THE END
IN MIND.

WHAT DO YOU WANT TO HAVE ACHIEVED BY THE END
OF YOUR FIRST 100 DAYS?

FOR EACH OF THE 10 CONSTITUENT ROLES, ACROSS
YOUR 'WHOLE SYSTEM' DECIDE WHAT YOU WANT TO
HAVE ACHIEVED BY END OF THE FIRST 100 DAYS,
AND THEN FILL IN THE FIRST100ASSIST™ TEMPLATE
WITH YOUR 10 DESIRED OUTCOMES.

PLEASE SEE EXAMPLES IN BLUE FOR A NEWLY APPOINTED MANAGING DIRECTOR OF "BUSINESS MARKETS":

THE PERSON (YOU, AS LEADER)

01 TRANSITION MAKER – WHAT IS YOUR LEADERSHIP SKILLS STEP UP?
DESIRED OUTCOME: BY THE END OF THE FIRST 100 DAYS, MY DESIRED OUTCOME ON TRANSITION MAKER IS TO HAVE ACHIEVED THE FOLLOWING…

_____

_____

_____

FOR EXAMPLE: MADE AN EFFECTIVE TRANSITION FROM MANAGING 500 PEOPLE TO LEADING A TEAM OF 3,000.

02 UNIQUE CONTRIBUTOR – WHAT UNIQUE ATTRIBUTES OR STRENGTHS CAN YOU CAPITALISE ON FOR THE BENEFIT OF EVERYBODY?
DESIRED OUTCOME: BY THE END OF THE FIRST 100 DAYS, MY DESIRED OUTCOME ON UNIQUE CONTRIBUTOR IS TO HAVE ACHIEVED THE FOLLOWING…

_____

_____

_____

FOR EXAMPLE: CAPITALISED ON MY COMMUNICATIONS STRENGTH TO REACH OUT AND INSPIRE MY ENTIRE GROUP OF 3,000. RE-ENERGISED THE "BUSINESS MARKETS" DIVISION AND HELP PEOPLE FEEL MORE CONNECTED TO COMPANY VISION AND MISSION.

CHAPTER 01: PREPARE

THE ROLE

03 CONTENT LEARNER – WHAT IS YOUR LEARNING CURVE/CONTENT KNOWLEDGE GAP?

DESIRED OUTCOME: BY THE END OF THE FIRST 100 DAYS, MY DESIRED OUTCOME ON CONTENT LEARNER IS TO HAVE ACHIEVED THE FOLLOWING…

FOR EXAMPLE: TACKLED THE INITIAL CONTENT/KNOWLEDGE LEARNING CURVE ON COMPANY STRATEGY AND "BUSINESS MARKETS" PRODUCTS AND SERVICES.

04 BUSINESS ACHIEVER – WHAT ARE YOUR KEY ROLE DELIVERABLES?

DESIRED OUTCOME: BY THE END OF THE FIRST 100 DAYS, MY DESIRED OUTCOME ON BUSINESS ACHIEVER IS TO HAVE ACHIEVED THE FOLLOWING…

FOR EXAMPLE:
– DELIVERED HIGH IMPACT QUICK WIN ON "BUSINESS MARKETS" STRATEGY
– IMPROVED "BUSINESS MARKETS" PROCESSES AND TEAM.
– GAINED GREATER INSIGHT INTO MAJOR BUSINESS CUSTOMERS: COMPLETED NEW SEGMENTATION ANALYSIS. (NOTE: I WOULD EXPECT MORE THAN ONE DESIRED OUTCOME FOR 'BUSINESS ACHIEVER' BECAUSE THESE ARE THE VERY TANGIBLE DELIVERABLES ASSOCIATED WITH YOUR ROLE CONTRIBUTION).

05 TEAM BUILDER – WHAT CAN YOU DO TO BUILD A HIGH PERFORMING TEAM?
DESIRED OUTCOME: BY THE END OF THE FIRST 100 DAYS, MY DESIRED OUTCOME
ON TEAM BUILDER IS TO HAVE ACHIEVED THE FOLLOWING…

_____

_____

_____

FOR EXAMPLE: RESTRUCTURED THE TEAM, REPLACED THE MARKETING DIRECTOR,
RE-ASSIGNED ROLES AND RESPONSIBILITIES.

**06 COMMUNICATIONS PROVIDER – WHAT COMMUNICATIONS ARCHITECTURE
WILL WORK FOR YOU IN THIS COMPANY?**
DESIRED OUTCOME: BY THE END OF THE FIRST 100 DAYS, MY DESIRED OUTCOME
ON COMMUNICATIONS PROVIDER IS TO HAVE ACHIEVED THE FOLLOWING…

_____

_____

_____

FOR EXAMPLE: ROLE PROGRESS AND PLANS COMMUNICATED TO TEAM
AND KEY STAKEHOLDERS, USING COMBINATION OF NEW INTRANET SITE, BLOG,
1 TO 1's, "TOWN HALLS".

CHAPTER 01: PREPARE

THE ORGANISATION

07 VALUE ADDER – WHAT IS YOUR VISION FOR THE ROLE, AND HOW CAN THIS
CREATE EXTRA VALUE FOR THE COMPANY?
DESIRED OUTCOME: BY THE END OF THE FIRST 100 DAYS, MY DESIRED OUTCOME
ON VALUE ADDER IS TO HAVE ACHIEVED THE FOLLOWING…

FOR EXAMPLE: REFRESHED THE VISION FOR "BUSINESS MARKETS" DIVISION:
AND SET OUT CLEAR DIRECTION ON NEXT 12 MONTH PRIORITIES.

08 RELATIONSHIP BUILDER – WHO REALLY MATTERS HERE? WHO ARE YOUR
ROLE STAKEHOLDERS?
DESIRED OUTCOME: BY THE END OF THE FIRST 100 DAYS, MY DESIRED OUTCOME
ON RELATIONSHIP BUILDER IS TO HAVE ACHIEVED THE FOLLOWING…

FOR EXAMPLE: MET MY TOP 10 STAKEHOLDERS, AND FORGED STRONG
EARLY RELATIONSHIPS.

09 CULTURE NAVIGATOR – WHAT DO YOU NEED TO DO TO SUCCESSFULLY NAVIGATE THIS CULTURE?
DESIRED OUTCOME: BY THE END OF THE FIRST 100 DAYS, MY DESIRED OUTCOME ON CULTURE NAVIGATOR IS TO HAVE ACHIEVED THE FOLLOWING…

FOR EXAMPLE: GAINED A BETTER UNDERSTANDING OF MY ENVIRONMENT: HOW THE POWER AND POLITICS OPERATE, HOW DECISIONS ARE MADE HERE.

THE MARKET

10 MARKET PLAYER – WHAT CAN YOU ACHIEVE IN TERMS OF A MARKET QUICK-WIN OR MAJOR IMPACT?
DESIRED OUTCOME: BY THE END OF THE FIRST 100 DAYS, MY DESIRED OUTCOME ON MARKET PLAYER IS TO HAVE ACHIEVED THE FOLLOWING…

FOR EXAMPLE: ANNOUNCED A RECESSION INSIGHT/FAST PROPOSITION INTO THE "BUSINESS MARKETS" MARKET PLACE.

STEP 2:
BREAK DOWN DESIRED OUTCOMES INTO @30, @60, @90 MILESTONES.

HAVING SET OUT YOUR LIST OF 10 DESIRED OUTCOMES, THE NEXT STEP IS TO BREAK DOWN EACH DESIRED OUTCOME INTO MONTHLY MILESTONES OF 30 DAYS/60 DAYS/90 DAYS PRECEDED BY INITIAL FIRST STEP ACTIONS.

See the First100™ Plan template on the next page. Use the template to write your First 100 Days Plan. Set out a page per each of your Desired Outcome.

For each Desired Outcome, list the first steps to be taken, and list the interim outcomes to be achieved by each 30 day milestone.

First step actions:
This is the list of first step activities/actions you need to take.
– Taking each Desired Outcome, one at a time, what do you need to do as first steps?

MONTHLY MILESTONE OUTCOMES:
THESE ARE NOT ACTIVITIES OR ACTIONS YOU NEED TO TAKE. THESE ARE OUTCOMES YOU WANT TO HAVE ACHIEVED BY EACH MILESTONE TO KNOW YOU ARE ON TRACK TO ACHIEVING YOUR DESIRED OUTCOME BY THE END OF 100 DAYS.

BY END OF 30 DAYS
– WHAT WOULD I NEED TO HAVE ACHIEVED BY END OF 30 DAYS, TO KNOW I AM ON TRACK TO ACHIEVING MY DESIRED OUTCOME BY END OF 100 DAYS. (FILL IN THE 'BY END 30 DAYS' BOX)

BY END OF 60 DAYS
– WHAT WOULD HAVE TO BE ACHIEVED BY END OF 60 DAYS, TO KNOW I AM ON TRACK TO ACHIEVING MY DESIRED OUTCOME BY END OF 100 DAYS. (FILL IN THE 'BY END 60 DAYS' BOX)

BY END OF 90 DAYS
– WHAT WOULD HAVE TO BE ACHIEVED BY END OF 90 DAYS, TO KNOW I AM ON TRACK TO ACHIEVING MY DESIRED OUTCOME BY END OF 100 DAYS. (FILL IN THE 'BY END 90 DAYS' BOX)

CHAPTER 01: PREPARE

FIRST100ASSIST™ TEMPLATE

01 TRANSITION MAKER – WHAT IS YOUR LEADERSHIP SKILLS STEP UP?
DESIRED OUTCOME: BY THE END OF THE FIRST 100 DAYS, MY DESIRED OUTCOME
ON TRANSITION MAKER IS TO HAVE ACHIEVED THE FOLLOWING…

FIRST STEPS	BY END 30 DAYS	BY END 60 DAYS	BY END 90 DAYS

Your First100™ Plan should have a page per each of your 10 Desired Outcomes, with space to fill your First Steps, and your 30/60/90 outcomes. When you have finished you will have a neat 10 page First100™ 10-point Plan document.

01 TRANSITION MAKER – WHAT IS YOUR LEADERSHIP SKILLS STEP UP?

02 UNIQUE CONTRIBUTOR – WHAT UNIQUE ATTRIBUTES OR STRENGTHS CAN YOU CAPITALISE ON FOR THE BENEFIT OF EVERYBODY?

03 CONTENT LEARNER – WHAT IS YOUR LEARNING CURVE/CONTENT KNOWLEDGE GAP?

04 BUSINESS ACHIEVER – WHAT ARE YOUR KEY ROLE DELIVERABLES?

05 TEAM BUILDER – WHAT CAN YOU DO TO BUILD A HIGH PERFORMING TEAM?

06 COMMUNICATIONS PROVIDER – WHAT COMMUNICATIONS ARCHITECTURE WILL WORK FOR YOU IN THIS COMPANY?

07 VALUE ADDER – WHAT IS YOUR VISION FOR THE ROLE, AND HOW CAN THIS CREATE EXTRA VALUE FOR THE COMPANY?

08 RELATIONSHIP BUILDER – WHO REALLY MATTERS HERE? WHO ARE YOUR ROLE STAKEHOLDERS?

09 CULTURE NAVIGATOR – WHAT DO YOU NEED TO DO TO SUCCESSFULLY NAVIGATE THIS CULTURE?

10 MARKET PLAYER – WHAT CAN YOU ACHIEVE IN TERMS OF A MARKET QUICK-WIN OR MAJOR IMPACT?

CHAPTER 01: PREPARE

TWO YEAR ROLE OBJECTIVES

ON VISION & STRATEGY	01 TRANSITION MAKER
	02 UNIQUE CONTRIBUTOR
	03 CONTENT LEARNER
	04 BUSINESS ACHIEVER
ON PEOPLE & TEAM	05 TEAM BUILDER
	06 COMMUNICATIONS PROVIDER
	07 VALUE ADDER
ON RESULTS & DELIVERABLES	08 RELATIONSHIP BUILDER
	09 CULTURE NAVIGATOR
	10 MARKET PLAYER

DESIRED OUTCOMES BY END OF FIRST 100 DAYS

STEP 3: SENSE-CHECK AND COMPLETE THE PLAN.

STOP AND CHECK, IS THERE ANYTHING YOU WOULD WANT TO PRIORITISE IN THE FIRST 100 DAYS THAT FOR ANY REASON IS NOT YET IN YOUR PLAN? IF SO, THINK ABOUT WHY? IS IT SIMPLY A TASK EN ROUTE TO ACHIEVING ONE OF THE DESIRED OUTCOMES? OR – HAVE YOU SIMPLY FORGOTTEN TO INCLUDE IT AND IT NEEDS TO GO IN NOW.

NOTE! PLEASE NOTE THE DIFFERENCE BETWEEN AN OUTCOME AND AN ACTION. FIRST STEPS ARE ABOUT ACTIONS. BUT MONTHLY MILESTONES ARE ABOUT OUTCOMES.

CHAPTER 02: @START
ESTABLISH YOURSELF AS LEADER

YOUR CHALLENGE IS ONLY JUST BEGINNING.

By now, you should have a great First 100 Days Plan. You are well prepared, the plan is thorough, it is aligned to stakeholder expectations and it is a great looking document to give to your new boss on arrival Day 1. So far, so good!

But of course, on arrival into the first day in the role, your challenge is only just beginning. You now need to bring your First 100 Days Plan to life, and execute it successfully. In order to do so, let's focus on you as a leader and on your ability to chart the course successfully.

MANAGER VERSUS LEADER

We have already mentioned the word 'leader' several times so far in this book. It's time now to clarify what is meant by this over-used and misunderstood term.

In my experience most business executives including Directors and CEOs of major global corporations are professional managers not leaders. You may believe you are a leader, you may have been told for years at your company that you are a leader, but I have rarely met anybody who is a real leader.

Most executives are professional managers; and by that I mean they rely on the power and authority of the role to get things done. Like managers they usually take up their role as someone involved in organising and marshalling resources in service of a task passed to them by another.

THAT'S A MANAGER, A FOLLOWER, NOT A LEADER.

CHAPTER 02: @START

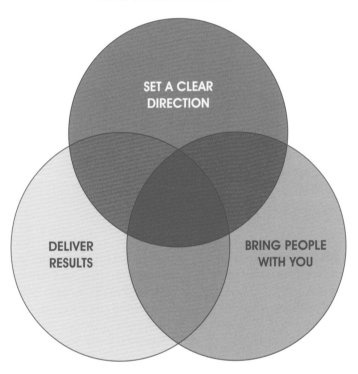

WHAT WOULD A LEADER DO?

SET A CLEAR
DIRECTION

DELIVER
RESULTS

BRING PEOPLE
WITH YOU

Thousands of books have been written on the subject of leadership.
They speak of Vision, Strategy, People, Teams, Values, Culture etc.
It gets very complicated. I like to keep it simple.

A LEADER MUST: – SET A CLEAR DIRECTION.
                  – BRINGS PEOPLE WITH HIM/HER.
                  – DELIVER RESULTS.

That's it! In your first 100 days – and beyond – keep in mind those 3 simple
things. Set a clear direction, bring people with you, and deliver early results.

SET A CLEAR DIRECTION:
No one knows the right answer about the future. But a leader will have the courage to put stakes in the ground and say 'I don't have the answer either, but let's go there'. 'There' could be a new market, could be new products and services, and could be a total rebrand or all of the aforementioned. It doesn't matter what 'there' is – the Leader has the guts to go for it. If 'there' is a very complicated point b, then a leader will understand that getting there will be complicated too and resistance will occur.

So you have to be very clear on the direction, and very clear on why you are going there. The more clarity on the end point, and the plan to get to the end point, then of course the easier the journey will be for everyone to get there.

'I DON'T HAVE THE ANSWER EITHER, BUT LET'S GO THERE'.

CHAPTER 02: @START

BRING PEOPLE WITH YOU:
Of course, if only the Leader goes 'there': nothing much has happened in terms of progress. The leader has to communicate his/her vision on 'there' to the people, and motivate them to come with him/her.

Never underestimate how much you have to keep communicating your direction, and the reasons for your direction, to others. Even when you don't know all the answers, keep communicating. And, of course, this is not one man trying to move a mountain, people will spontaneously follow you when they understand and believe in you.

COMMUNICATION, COMMUNICATION, COMMUNICATION.

DELIVER RESULTS:
Reaching 'there' and all the efforts invested to get 'there' will
only have been a good idea and a good plan if results prove
it. Otherwise, we all realise the leader made a big mistake on
direction and we were foolish to follow. The delivery of results
demonstrates the quality of the leader in terms of ability to set
a clear direction and bring the people with him.

I could write a separate book on each of these 3 aspects,
but I won't. I am deliberately keeping it this simple, and I do
so with my clients – because everything else is just noise.

IF YOU WANT ACCELERATED SUCCESS IN YOUR FIRST
100 DAYS, YOU KEEP IT SIMPLE TOO.

– SET A CLEAR DIRECTION ON WHERE YOU WANT
TO BE BY THE END OF 100 DAYS.

– BRING YOUR TEAM, STAKEHOLDERS AND PEOPLE
WITH YOU.

– DELIVER RESULTS BY THE END OF THE FIRST
100 DAYS.

CHAPTER 02: @START
LAUNCH YOUR FIRST 100 DAYS PLAN

You can make a fanfare launch of your First 100 Day Plan as soon as you arrive, but my advice is that it is best to ground yourself in the role for 5-10 days to check what the experience is like on arrival, and to confirm and make any final tweaks to the plan.

For example, prior to arrival, you may not yet have met the key stakeholders, so your 100 day plan will not have included all stakeholder expectations.

ON ARRIVAL, I RECOMMEND THE FOLLOWING STEPS:
– CHECK/RECONFIRM KEY ROLE STAKEHOLDERS, AND THEIR EXPECTATION OF YOU.

– MEET YOUR DIRECT REPORT TEAM, AND GET UP TO SPEED ON THEIR CURRENT CHALLENGES.

– PHYSICALLY LAND INTO THE BUILDING AND ORGANISATION TO GET YOUR OWN SENSE OF THE PLACE.

TO WHO?

WHETHER OR NOT TO COMMUNICATE YOUR PLAN
TO ALL ROLE STAKEHOLDERS IS UP TO YOU.
I RECOMMEND THAT YOU SHARE IT FULLY WITH YOUR
BOSS, BUT AFTER THAT YOU MAY CHOOSE TACTICALLY
HOW MUCH OF THE PLAN TO SHARE, AND WHO
WITH, DEPENDING ON WHAT IS APPROPRIATE TO
YOUR CONTEXT.

AND HOW?

HOW YOU COMMUNICATE YOUR PLAN IS ANOTHER
MATTER. WHILST IT WAS USEFUL FOR YOU TO
CONSTRUCT YOUR PLAN ON PAPER, IN TERMS OF
COMMUNICATION TO OTHERS YOU MAY WISH TO
AVAIL OF THE FULL SUITE OF COMMUNICATION
ARCHITECTURE AVAILABLE: FOR EXAMPLE. IN
PERSON, ROADSHOWS, TOWNHALLS, PODCAST,
BLOGS, EMAIL, PAPER, AND/OR ANY OTHER
EFFECTIVE MEANS FOR YOUR CONTEXT.

CHAPTER 02: @START
KNOW THAT EQ IS AS IMPORTANT AS IQ

Having launched your First 100 Days Plan, how are you going to bring others with you on the plan and 100 day journey?

THE SHORT ANSWER IS THAT YOUR EQ WILL BE AS IMPORTANT AS YOUR IQ.

The analytical mindset of the business executive plays tricks and creates a convenient illusion that an organisation can be controlled and managed as a set of systems, processes, and organisation charts. First 100 Day Plans, whilst necessary to attempt to gain control in the first 100 days, play into this illusion – but in the end, remember that organisations are simply highly interpersonal places.

Organisations are all about people and how they relate to each other. Whilst we emphasise the importance of having a First 100 Days Plan, we don't underestimate the importance of your EQ skills in being able to bring the Plan to life with others.

IT IS ALL ABOUT PEOPLE AND HOW THEY RELATE TO EACH OTHER.

EQ REFERS TO EMOTIONAL INTELLIGENCE: SELF-AWARENESS, SELF-REGULATION, SELF-MOTIVATION, EMPATHY AND SOCIAL SKILL.

Being fit for purpose on Emotional Intelligence will be a very important aspect of the 'how' on your first 100 days plan.

The viral, emotional, interpersonal life of the organisation will be an important factor to synthesise, diagnose and understand. Plus as Leader you will be in a strong position to affect, lead and guide people towards a positive new emotional resonance if you are well equipped emotionally to do so. Having the right advisory support systems in place to sense-check both your intellectual choices and emotional choices will serve you well in your first 100 days.

CHAPTER 02: @START

The first 100 days is an intense time period so naturally your emotional reactions will be heightened. This is an issue and in particular, you need to develop self-awareness to observe when these heightened emotions are taking over, and you need to exercise self-regulation to manage and overcome these emotions.

For example, you may feel extremely buoyant and optimistic in the first few weeks of the first 100 days – and these feelings may exaggerate themselves to the extent that you lose touch with commercial reality and over-promise on delivery of year end results. Your team won't thank you for this!

Or you may feel anxious at the beginning of the first 100 days - and if you are not able to manage the anxiety, then you are more likely to postpone decision-making. This will not enhance your leadership reputation, and others may lose confidence in you.

My advice is to be open to the hypothesis that no matter who you are, no matter how experienced, you will have exaggerated reactions to what is happening around you in the first 100 days of a role appointment. Be open to the idea that these emotions may range from the panic/fear/overwhelm end of the spectrum to the overconfident/ arrogant end of the spectrum – and everything in-between, and that you may be in danger of 'acting out' accordingly.

Realise that how you handle your emotions
during the first 100 days – particularly at the start
- will be a critical factor for your performance
acceleration. Get it wrong, and you may alienate
others early. Get it right, and you will make more
accelerated progress.

To keep your emotions under check, I would
recommend practising humility. Remember,
you are still the same person you were the
day before you were appointed. Nothing has
materially changed in you, but the stakes have
got higher. Hopefully accepting this will make
you realise that you are under more pressure
than usual, and that you need to be even
calmer than usual as a result. Stay balanced.

CHAPTER 02: @START
THE FIVE FACTORS OF SUCCESS

Having worked with many leaders during their first 100 days, I developed a view on what were the critical success factors. Now that you are at the start of your first 100 days, it is the time to share them with you.

01 BRING FORWARD A CLEAR VISION

Following on from what I mentioned re Leading versus Managing, the Leader in the first 100 days, has to bring forward a clear vision. Even if a vision has already been set by the predecessor, I always say to clients what's the point of having you in the job versus anybody else if you can't add, build, refresh or reinvent the vision. So, what is your vision? To put it another way, when you leave the role, what do you want people to say is your legacy. It's another way of starting with the end in mind – think about leaving the role, and what you want to have left behind. Then you can set out your vision.

WHAT IS YOUR VISION?

CHAPTER 02: @START

02 HAVE NO FEAR (BE CONFIDENT)

I have noticed that everybody – regardless of seniority or experience – suffers a confidence loss in the first 100 days. This is natural, and I legitimise this feeling with clients – after all, they have never done this role before, so of course confidence is an issue.

Confidence is very important, because you need to be able to make good decisions and not panic in the overwhelm of the first 100 days. 'Fear' is the great enemy of confidence. Fear paralyses performance. But please remember that fear is only imagination about something that has not actually happened. Our thoughts create reality, so cancel all fear thoughts from the mind and replace them with confident thoughts. If you are gripped with fear, speak with your rational self to say that fear is just imaginary and you can choose to imagine a positive outcome instead.

ANOTHER TECHNIQUE IS TO IMAGINE A FIRE AND EVERY TIME A FEAR-THOUGHT COMES INTO YOUR MIND, PUT IT INTO THE FIRE AND WATCH IT BURN.

'FEAR' IS THE GREAT ENEMY OF CONFIDENCE. FEAR PARALYSES PERFORMANCE.

03 EXERCISE PATIENCE AND RESILIENCE

A leader in a new role is psyched up to perform and make changes as fast as possible given their new authority and mandate.

Unfortunately resistance to change appears to be the status quo of even the best organisations. So, be realistic that while you are in gung-ho mode, your team and those around you may be suffering change fatigue and may be both consciously and unconsciously resistant to your ideas. Accept that resistance to change is the more likely situation and devise strategies for overcoming these resistances. In other words, try not to get frustrated by the slow pace of others, instead accept that (unfortunately) it is the human condition to resist change – but at the same time work to overcome it.

Be patient with yourself and with others.

BE PATIENT AND RESILIENT IN THE FACE OF CHALLENGES AND OBSTACLES.

04 BE A FAST LEARNER

The industry, market and organisation will keep on moving, and there is no pause whilst you get up to speed in your first 100 days. So you have to be committed and able to learn as fast as possible. This is why I suggested earlier that you negotiate extra latitude and time from loved ones, so that during the first 100 days you are fully focussed on narrowing content gaps and learning the ropes as fast as possible.

05 DON'T BE AFRAID OF YOUR MISTAKES

We all make mistakes. That is never going to change. So don't be afraid to make mistakes. Mistakes are a rich source of learning and make up the sum of our total experience and wisdom. The important thing about mistakes is how you handle them – very often a mistake can be an opportunity to build a deeper relationship with someone we work with because those around you may be very forgiving of early mistakes.

You have to move forward with courage and without perfect information so it is inevitable that mistakes will be made – so just accept it, and don't worry about it!

II. MIDDLE

THE HARD WORK STARTS NOW.

You need to go deeper now, move beyond your self and get others working for you. 'Middle' is about staying the course and putting extra energy and effort into achieving your initiatives. 'Middle' phase is that moment in the marathon when you may feel you are up against a wall, and a feeling that you may have bitten off more than you can chew. Same with taking on a new role. But know that if you keep persevering then glory awaits you. In the first 30 days you will be forgiven for spending most of your time meeting your boss and team and getting up to speed.

But in this phase, that early understanding starts to give way to desire from your role stakeholders to see real action occurring and early results secured.

The most important thing to do right now is to stop, take stock, and review progress against where you expected to be 30 days into your 100 day plan.

WE ALL KNOW YOU HAVE BEEN BUSY, BUT HAVE YOU BEEN BUSY DOING THE RIGHT THINGS?

Since arriving, no doubt but that external factors have kicked in, or the situation is worse/different/better than envisaged. Stay focussed on your 100 day plan. Derailment from the strategic priorities is what stops executives making an impact in the first 100 days. This @30 day mark represents a key milestone opportunity to take stock of progress and check whether you have fallen into the trap of low level detail or fire-fighting or other distractions. Its time to dust off your 100 day plan – especially if you haven't looked at it in a while!

ARE YOU STAYING FOCUSSED ON YOUR KEY PRIORITIES?

Have you achieved what you wanted by this point, in service of your desired outcomes by the end of the first 100 days? What are you spending time on? If you are spending time on activities not on the Plan, then ask yourself why? You either adjust the Plan or stop doing them.

REVIEW PROGRESS AGAINST PLAN @30 DAYS

REVIEW YOUR DESIRED OUTCOMES FOR THE FIRST 100 DAYS.

TAKE STOCK ON WHAT IS WORKING WELL/NOT WELL WITH YOUR PLAN.

AT HIGH LEVEL, ARE YOU ON TRACK TO ACHIEVING THOSE DESIRED OUTCOMES?
IF NOT, WHY NOT?
– BRAINSTORM SOLUTIONS TO ANY BLOCKS/ CHALLENGES.
– THINK ABOUT THE PERFORMANCE ACCELERATION OPPORTUNITIES.
– WHO CAN HELP.

AT DETAILED LEVEL, REVIEW EACH DESIRED OUTCOME AND RESET THE ACTIONS FOR THE NEXT 30 DAYS.

@30 DAYS CHECKLIST.

HOW DID YOU SPEND YOUR OWN TIME AND ENERGY IN THE FIRST 30 DAYS?

YOU CANNOT DO EVERYTHING, BUT MAKING THE RIGHT CHOICES ON HOW YOU SPEND YOUR DAY TO DAY TIME AT DIFFERENT STAGES IN THE FIRST 100 DAYS WILL BE IMPORTANT – IN BOTH SYMBOLIC AND REAL TERMS. AS A SYMBOLIC INDICATOR, IT RE-ENFORCES YOUR 100 DAY PRIORITIES BECAUSE OTHERS SEE THAT YOU 'WALK THE TALK' AND THIS GIVES THEM THE MOTIVATION TO ACT ACCORDINGLY. IT IS ALSO VERY REAL BECAUSE IF YOU ARE A PERSON OF SUBSTANCE AND IF YOU INVEST TIME AND ATTENTION IN A PARTICULAR AREA THEN IT WILL CERTAINLY REAP A TANGIBLE MEASURABLE DIVIDEND BECAUSE OF YOUR FOCUS AND INVOLVEMENT.

CHAPTER 03: @30 DAYS

DID YOU MANAGE THE OVERWHELM, AND RISE ABOVE THE SEA OF 'WELL WISHERS'?	DURING THE FIRST 30 DAYS, YOU WILL HAVE A LOT OF NEW PEOPLE TO MEET, AND TO DEAL WITH – BOTH EXTERNALLY AND INTERNALLY. EVERYBODY PROBABLY WANTS A 'PIECE' OF YOU, AND THAT CAN BE OVERWHELMING. YOUR ABILITY TO JUDGE WHO IS VALUABLE, WHO IS AUTHENTIC, WHO IS RELIABLE, WHO CAN DELIVER, WILL BE CRUCIAL IN ACCELERATING 100 DAY PRIORITIES AND PLANS.
DID YOU STRIKE THE RIGHT BALANCE BETWEEN MOVING TOO FAST, AND MOVING TOO SLOWLY?	YOU WANT TO MOVE WITH SPEED, IN AN ORGANISATION THAT MOVES VERY SLOWLY. FINDING THE RIGHT CALIBRATION DURING THE FIRST 100 DAYS BETWEEN MOVING TOO FAST, AND MOVING TOO SLOW, WILL REQUIRE THOUGHTFULNESS AND CONSIDERATION.
HOW DID YOU DEAL WITH YOUR PREDECESSOR?	HOW YOU DEAL WITH YOUR PREDECESSOR IN THE FIRST 30 DAYS WILL BE IMPORTANT AND SEND SIGNALS AS TO HOW YOU DEAL WITH PEOPLE. REGARDLESS OF WHETHER YOUR PREDECESSOR DID A GOOD JOB OR NOT, THE RIGHT THING TO DO IS TO THANK THEM PUBLICLY AND THEN FULLY TAKE OVER.

HOW DID YOU RESPOND TO FIRST MISTAKES/BAD NEWS/ EARLY PRESSURE?	IT'S A BIT LIKE AN EARLY COURTSHIP IN THE FIRST 100 DAYS. AS SUCH EVERYBODY WANTS TO PLEASE AND IMPRESS EVERYBODY ELSE. BUT BEING HUMANS, IT IS INEVITABLE THAT MISTAKES WILL BE MADE, AND THAT MISUNDERSTANDINGS WILL ARISE. YOU WILL MAKE MISTAKES. YOUR PEOPLE WILL MAKE MISTAKES. NO MATTER HOW EXPERIENCED, WRONG TURNS ARE INEVITABLE. HOW YOU RECOVER FROM WRONG TURNS, HOW YOU HANDLE YOURSELF AND OTHERS DURING THE HEIGHTENED STRESS PERIOD OF THE FIRST 100 DAYS WILL BE IMPORTANT. HAVING A SET OF 'PRESSURE-VALVE-RELEASE' SYSTEMS IN PLACE IN THE FIRST 100 DAYS CAN BE CRUCIAL TO SUCCESS.
HOW WELL HAVE YOU COPED WITH THE UNKNOWNS, AND AVOIDED DERAILMENT?	IT IS QUITE NORMAL THAT A FIRST 100 DAY PLAN DOESN'T HAVE CONTINGENCY FOR UNKNOWNS – GIVEN THAT 'UNKNOWNS' ARE HARD TO CATER FOR IN A PLAN (!). FOR EXAMPLE, MACRO EXTERNAL FACTORS MAY COME MORE INTO PLAY. AND/OR MORE MICRO ISSUES MAY COME INTO PLAY.

CHAPTER 03: @30 DAYS

HAVE YOU A SENSE AS TO WHETHER YOU HAVE THE RIGHT PEOPLE IN THE RIGHT ROLES?	HAVING EXPLAINED THE 'WHAT' TO YOUR PEOPLE, PERHAPS THEY WILL STRUGGLE ON THE 'HOW'. HAVING SMART, DRIVEN, AGILE PEOPLE AROUND YOU WILL BE VERY IMPORTANT. THIS MAY TAKE A DISPROPORTIONATE AMOUNT OF TIME UPFRONT IN THE FIRST 100 DAYS TO REALISE WHO REALLY IS "ON THE BUS" WITH YOU – AND YOU WILL NEED TO CONTINUE TO SENSE-CHECK IT FROM TIME TO TIME.
HOW WELL ARE YOU COMMUNICATING YOUR 100 DAY PLAN?	COMMUNICATE, COMMUNICATE, COMMUNICATE. HOW YOU COMMUNICATE YOUR PLAN WILL MAKE OR BREAK THE MOBILISATION OF OTHERS IN TERMS OF DELIVERING THE PLAN. YOU MAY NEED TO FIND SEVERAL WAYS OF SAYING THE SAME THING. INSTALLING AND LEVERAGING THE RIGHT BREADTH AND DEPTH OF 'COMMUNICATION ARCHITECTURE' IS A CRITICAL AREA OF IMPORTANCE FOR FIRST 100 DAY SUCCESS.

HOW ARE YOU DEALING WITH YOUR BOSS AND/OR BOARD?	THE RELATIONSHIP BETWEEN YOU AND YOUR BOSS IN PARTICULAR IS ONE THAT NEEDS ATTENTION AND CARE DURING THE FIRST 100 DAYS.
ARE YOU CELEBRATING YOUR SUCCESSES, AND HAVING FUN ALONG THE WAY?	YOUR FIRST 100 DAYS WILL BE INTENSE, SO IT IS VERY IMPORTANT TO FACTOR IN TIME FOR 'PAUSING', TAKING STOCK, CELEBRATING SUCCESSES ON THE JOURNEY. THE FIRST 100 DAYS IS LIKE A SPRINT AND THE REST OF THE FIRST 12 MONTHS IS LIKE A MARATHON. AT ALL STAGES, BUT PARTICULARLY IN THE SPRINT STAGE, YOU WILL WANT TO ENSURE THAT YOU FEEL FULFILLED THROUGHOUT THE WHOLE EXPERIENCE SO THAT IT IS BOTH ENERGETIC AND ENERGISING.

CHAPTER 03: @30 DAYS
DECIDE WHO & WHAT REALLY MATTERS HERE

WITH 30 DAYS EXPERIENCE UNDER YOUR BELT,
NOW IS A GOOD TIME TO ASK YOURSELF:
– WHAT REALLY MATTERS HERE?
– WHO REALLY MATTERS HERE?

It takes time to work these nuances out. And that's why I'm bringing this up now – you have been busy getting started in the last 30 days, but now is the time to lift up your head again and think more deeply about these points.

Skilled political behaviour involves understanding how organisations work and mobilising resources to achieve the organisation's purposes. Achieving leaders realise that there are two dimensions at play in every relationship, every meeting, every department, every organisation:

WHAT IS HAPPENING 'ABOVE THE SURFACE', AND WHAT IS HAPPENING 'BELOW THE SURFACE'.

The ability to read the organisational world is very important skill, and you may have the greatest First 100 Days Plan in the world, but if you miss out on who and what really matters here, all your efforts will be in vain.

– DO YOU HAVE A FEEL FOR THE POWER BASES, OVERT AND COVERT AGENDAS, FORMAL AND INFORMAL NETWORKS?

– WHO ARE THE KEY DECISION-MAKERS, AND INFLUENCERS?

– DO YOU UNDERSTAND THE FORMAL ORGANISATION CHART, AND THE INFORMAL ORGANISATION CHART?

– THE WHO AND THE WHAT IS USUALLY NOT FORMALLY EXPLAINED OR WRITTEN DOWN, SO ARE YOU POLITICALLY AWARE ENOUGH TO READ BETWEEN THE LINES?

– IF YOU ARE NOT POLITICALLY SAVVY, THEN HOW ARE YOU GOING TO MITIGATE THIS?

Reading an organisation takes skill, time and sensitivity to other people. You need to get good at reading the political structure of the organisation and what makes it tick.

INVEST IN THE NETWORK NOW.

Don't just focus on the task at hand, my suggestion is that you reach out and invest time on understanding important relationships and networks too.

IN THE FIRST 30 DAYS, THE ATTENTION HAS BEEN ON YOU, BUT A LEADER CANNOT ACHIEVE ANYTHING WITHOUT A STRONG, HIGH PERFORMING TEAM.

BUILD THE HEALTH OF YOUR TEAM

I have found it works to think of the team using
the analogy of the 'body'; and within this frame,
a team is considered healthy (ie. high performing)
if the sum of the parts are a clear head (team
analytics, team intelligence, team knowledge),
capable hands (team skills, team competencies),
and a strong heart (team passion, team
motivation, team spirit).

I put it to you that each component part of the
'body' must be in place in order for the whole
'body' (team) to function effectively.

CHAPTER 03: @30 DAYS

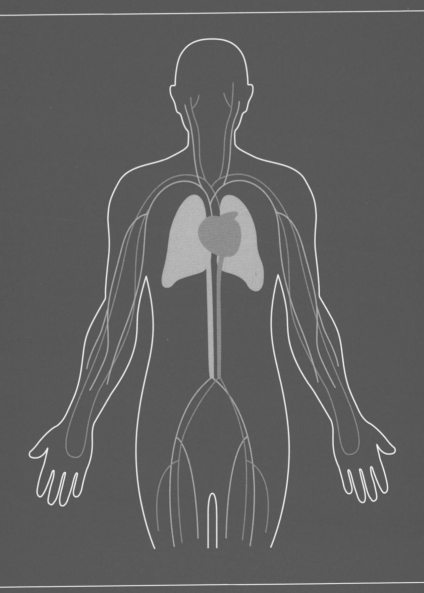

Step back and do a health check on your team. Does the sum of the parts make up a healthy team? For example, does the team have the intelligence (head), the skills (hands), but lacks the passion (heart) for high performance?

IDEAS FOR BUILDING THE HEALTH OF YOUR TEAM MAY INCLUDE:

– INVEST IN SKILLS TRAINING.

– INVEST IN TEAM BUILDING.

– RECRUIT TO FILL THE GAPS.

CHAPTER 03: @30 DAYS

**DO YOU HAVE THE RIGHT PEOPLE IN
THE RIGHT ROLES?**
If the previous insight was about the sum of
the parts, we suggest you also examine the
individual parts.

By 30 days, you have a lot more personal
experience and information on what needs
to be achieved, the likely challenges ahead,
and the quality of the team around you.

– DO YOU HAVE THE RIGHT PEOPLE IN THE RIGHT
ROLES?

– WHAT CHANGES NEED TO BE MADE NOW OR
NEED TO BE PLANNED FOR LATER?

– WHAT, IF ANYTHING, IS MISSING IN THE CONTEXT
OF THE GOALS YOU WANT TO ACHIEVE?

– DO YOU NEED TO BRING FRESH TALENT AND
ENERGY FROM ELSEWHERE IN THE ORGANISATION
OR HIRE EXTERNALLY?

AND IN MY EXPERIENCE, THE ANSWER TO THE LATTER
QUESTION IS ALWAYS A RESOUNDING...

...YES.

YOU HAVE TO GIVE YOUR INHERITED PEOPLE A
CHANCE, BUT MOVING TOO SLOWLY ON PUTTING
THE RIGHT PEOPLE IN THE RIGHT ROLES CAN HAVE
A VERY NEGATIVE IMPACT ON PERFORMANCE
ACCELERATION IN THE FIRST 100 DAYS, AND
FIRST 12 MONTHS.

UPDATE YOUR FIRST 100 DAYS PLAN @30 DAYS.

Based on your first 30 days experience, and on:

– A REVIEW OF PROGRESS AGAINST PLAN,
AND @30 DAYS CHECKLIST.

– WHO & WHAT MATTERS HERE?

– OPPORTUNITIES TO FAST-FORWARD THE TEAM.

REVIEW PROGRESS AGAINST EACH DESIRED
OUTCOME AND RESET THE ACTIONS FOR THE
NEXT 30 DAYS.

STOP AGAIN, TAKE STOCK, AND REVIEW PROGRESS.

THE MOST IMPORTANT THING TO DO RIGHT NOW
IS TO STOP ACTIVITY, TAKE STOCK, AND REVIEW
PROGRESS AGAINST WHERE YOU EXPECTED TO BE
60 DAYS INTO YOUR 100 DAY PLAN.

AT 60 DAYS, YOU ARE MOST LIKELY TO HAVE
FORGOTTEN YOUR 100 DAY PLAN. MY GUESS IS THAT
YOU HAVE NO TIME, AND YOU MAY EVEN POST-
RATIONALISE THAT YOUR PLAN WAS FINE TO GET YOU
STARTED BUT THERE ARE BIGGER ISSUES AT PLAY NOW.

NOT TRUE. EVEN IF SOMEWHAT TRUE, NOT
ABSOLUTELY TRUE. STOP AND THINK AGAIN.

CHAPTER 04: @60 DAYS

It is even more important than ever to take stock and review your plan @60 days.

– ARE YOU STAYING FOCUSSED ON YOUR KEY 100 DAY PRIORITIES?

– HAVE YOU ACHIEVED WHAT YOU WANTED BY THIS POINT, IN SERVICE OF YOUR DESIRED OUTCOMES BY THE END OF THE FIRST 100 DAYS?

– WHAT ARE YOU SPENDING TIME ON?

– IF YOU ARE SPENDING TIME ON ACTIVITIES NOT ON THE PLAN, THEN ASK YOURSELF WHY? YOU EITHER ADJUST THE PLAN OR STOP DOING THEM.

REVIEW PROGRESS AGAINST PLAN @60 DAYS

REVIEW YOUR DESIRED OUTCOMES FOR THE FIRST
100 DAYS.

TAKE STOCK ON WHAT IS WORKING WELL/NOT WELL
WITH YOUR PLAN.

AT HIGH LEVEL, ARE YOU ON TRACK TO ACHIEVING
THOSE DESIRED OUTCOMES?
IF NOT, WHY NOT?
- BRAINSTORM SOLUTIONS TO ANY BLOCKS/
  CHALLENGES.
- THINK ABOUT THE PERFORMANCE ACCELERATION
  OPPORTUNITIES.
- WHO CAN HELP?

AT DETAILED LEVEL, REVIEW EACH DESIRED
OUTCOME AND RESET THE ACTIONS FOR THE NEXT
30 DAYS.

@60 DAYS CHECKLIST.

HAVE YOU MET ALL YOUR KEY STAKEHOLDERS YET?	WHO OF YOUR STAKEHOLDERS HAVE YOU MET TO DATE AND WHO DO YOU NEED TO ENSURE YOU MEET IN THE NEXT 30 - 40 DAYS?
WHAT ABOUT THE CEO?	HAVE YOU MET THE CEO YET, HEARD HIM OR HER SPEAK? DO YOU HAVE ANY SENSE OF HIS OR HER MISSION AND YOUR ROLE IN UNDERPINNING THAT MISSION?
HOW DO YOU FEEL RIGHT NOW?	ARE YOU TIRED, OVERWHELMED, NEED A SHORT BREAK IN ORDER TO RE-GAIN PERSPECTIVE? ALTERNATIVELY IF YOU DON'T FEEL PUSHED OR CHALLENGED, WHY IS THAT? WHAT IS IT THAT YOU ARE NOT DOING TO MAKE MORE OF AN EFFORT ON IMPACT IN THE FIRST 100 DAYS?
ARE YOU ON TRACK TO DELIVER REAL RESULTS?	IF I WERE TO MEET YOU IN THE CORRIDOR OF YOUR OFFICES, COULD YOU CONVINCE ME THAT YOU HAVE DELIVERED TANGIBLE RESULTS YET? AND/OR ARE MEASURABLE IMPACTFUL RESULTS ON TRACK TO BE ACHIEVED BY THE END OF YOUR FIRST 100 DAYS?

CHAPTER 04: @60 DAYS

HAVE YOU DEALT WITH YOUR PEOPLE ISSUES?	DO YOU HAVE A GOOD DIRECT REPORT TEAM UNDER YOU AND/OR AN ACTION PLAN IN PLACE TO IMPROVE THE PERFORMANCE OF YOUR DIRECT REPORT TEAM?
DO YOU HAVE THE NECESSARY BUDGET AND RESOURCES?	HAVE YOU SECURED THE BUDGET AND RESOURCES REQUIRED TO MAKE THE KIND OF IMPACT AND CHANGE NECESSARY TO DELIVER NOT ONLY ON YOUR FIRST 100 DAYS, BUT ALSO ON YOUR FIRST 12 MONTH PRIORITIES AND YOUR 2 YEAR VISION FOR THIS ROLE?
HOW MANY MISTAKES HAVE YOU MADE SO FAR? AND HAVE YOU CORRECTED THEM YET?	IF YOU CAN'T LIST AT LEAST FIVE, THEN YOU ARE NOT SELF-AWARE AND YOU MAY WANT TO CLOSE THE GAP ON BLIND SPOTS VERY QUICKLY BY SOLICITING THE HELP/VIEWS OF OTHERS AS TO WHAT COULD HAVE GONE BETTER.

ARE YOU LOOKING AFTER YOUR HEALTH AND ENERGY LEVELS?	REMEMBER WAY BACK WHEN YOU READ THE CHAPTER ON PREPARING FOR YOUR FIRST 100 DAYS? GO BACK AND REFRESH YOUR MEMORY ON THE ENERGY MANAGEMENT SYSTEM AND TAKE NECESSARY ACTIONS TO MAINTAIN/REGAIN INCREASED ENERGY FOR THE FINAL SURGE OF THE NEXT 30-40 DAYS.
HAVE YOU GENERATED ANY NEW ROLE INSIGHTS?	YOU HAVE BEEN IN THIS ROLE 60 DAYS NOW. YOU HAVE A LOT MORE INFORMATION AND EXPERIENCE ABOUT THIS ROLE, THE MAIN PLAYERS, THE MARKET, WHAT CAN BE REALISTICALLY ACHIEVED? YOU ARE WELL-POSITIONED TO STEP BACK AND REFLECT ON ANY NEW INSIGHTS REGARDING WHAT WOULD CONSTITUTE SUCCESS IN THIS ROLE.
ARE YOU AND YOUR BOSS ALIGNED?	IDEALLY YOU AND YOUR BOSS SHOULD BE A LINE OF ONE- IN TERMS OF WHAT NEEDS TO BE ACHIEVED AND HOW. EVEN IF YOU DIFFER ON APPROACH, IT IS IMPORTANT TO MAINTAIN ALIGNMENT WITH YOUR BOSS AS S/HE IS YOUR PRIMARY ADVOCATE RIGHT NOW. (AFTER ALL, S/HE HIRED YOU)

CHAPTER 04: @60 DAYS
MAKE FINAL DECISIONS ON WHO STAYS/ WHO GOES

By now you have 2 months experience of your team's performance. Under the 'Team Builder' section of your 100 day plan, you may have already re-organised the structure, re-assigned roles and responsibilities, and you may even have moved some folks on and brought in fresh, new talent.

However, in my experience, 60 days can go by in a flash and sometimes these tough personnel decisions have not been taken yet. Or, it may be the case that some decisions have been taken but not ALL decisions have been taken yet.

NOW IS THE TIME.

I suggest that now, in the spirit of moving quickly to achieve your aims, it is time to make any final lingering decisions on who stays/who goes.

REMIND YOURSELF OF YOUR ROLE MISSION, AND WHAT YOU WANT TO ACHIEVE WITHIN 2 YEARS, AND HOW YOU NEED TO GET OFF TO AN ACCELERATED START. AND THAT MEANS, YOU HAVE TO HAVE THE RIGHT TEAM IN PLACE WITH EVERYBODY ROWING IN THE RIGHT DIRECTION, AND EVERYBODY A FULLY SIGNED UP CONTRIBUTING MEMBER OF THE TEAM.

With that in mind, consider again your team - and, in particular, your direct report team. Consider their skills, experience and value-add – and their potential.

CAN YOU SPOT THE PERSON(S) WHO IS NOT A NET CONTRIBUTOR?

ie. the person who is 'consuming' more value than they are 'contributing' and who, realistically, no level of skills building or investment is going to give you the fast high net return that you require.

Nobody likes to let people go, but avoiding the issue is hardly helpful either.

Eventually you will have to make these tough personnel decisions, and in my experience it is better to make them early on.

Although I work with very senior executives, who think of themselves as hard-nosed business-minded leaders, these tough personnel calls seem to linger on and on. Unfortunately I am no longer ever surprised when the non-net-contributor is still in place not just after the 100 days, but even 12 months later.

DO YOURSELF AND DO THAT PERSON A FAVOUR - MAKE YOUR DECISION NOW ON WHO STAYS/WHO GOES.

THE MULTIPLIER EFFECT.

Having been in situ for 60 days, perhaps you already have an insight on the levers that will catapult you towards a successful end. My suggestion is that you capitalise on what I call the "multiplier effect".

AS THE LEADER OF THE TEAM, YOU HAVE A MULTIPLIER EFFECT – BOTH POTENTIALLY POSITIVE AND NEGATIVE.

In other words, people consciously and unconsciously mirror and copy the behaviours of the leader.

Identify an insight on your biggest performance gap/acceleration opportunity. If you focus on changing this one thing about yourself – a quality, a characteristic, a standard, behaviour, and a norm – it has an effect on all those around you.

By definition, a leader has followers. So if all those working for you consciously or unconsciously follow your lead, and everyone working for them will follow their lead, and so on, then the cascading effect is extremely powerful as a change mechanism and it starts with you!

The first 100 days is intense, and the middle phase is tiring as you get to grips with the detail of the role. So take a short break, if possible, because now is the time to regroup your energy levels, and get ready for the final surge.

THE END OF YOUR FIRST 100 DAYS IS IN SIGHT,

SO GO FOR IT!

UPDATE YOUR FIRST 100 DAYS PLAN @60 DAYS.

Based on your first 60 days experience, and on:

– A REVIEW OF PROGRESS AGAINST PLAN, AND @60
DAYS CHECKLIST.

– FINAL DECISIONS RE WHO STAYS/WHO GOES.

– HOW TO CAPITALISE ON THE MULTIPLIER EFFECT.

REVIEW PROGRESS AGAINST EACH DESIRED
OUTCOME AND RESET THE ACTIONS FOR THE NEXT
30 DAYS.

III. END

EVERY ENDING IS SIMPLY A NEW BEGINNING.

Psychologists say that endings are always psychologically painful, whether people are consciously aware of it or not. Taoists wisely say every ending is simply a new beginning.

When it comes to arriving at the end phase of your first 100 days, what I say to you is that you need to enjoy a positive ending. You have been around long enough for people to have formed a view on you – sense check that view and see it as valuable information for a renewed start after your first 100 days.

Reflect back to extract and learn lessons from the experience – celebrate the wins, mourn the missed opportunities, and then draw a line under it. Move forward into a whole new phase: the start of the rest of the first financial year in the role. That will be the next important moment of judgement on you.

TAKE STOCK AND REVIEW.

REVIEW PROGRESS AGAINST PLAN @90 DAYS

REVIEW YOUR DESIRED OUTCOMES FOR THE FIRST
100 DAYS.

TAKE STOCK ON WHAT IS WORKING WELL/NOT WELL
WITH YOUR PLAN.

AT HIGH LEVEL, ARE YOU ON TRACK TO ACHIEVING
THOSE DESIRED OUTCOMES?
IF NOT, WHY NOT?
– BRAINSTORM SOLUTIONS TO ANY BLOCKS/
  CHALLENGES.
– THINK ABOUT THE PERFORMANCE ACCELERATION
  OPPORTUNITIES.
– WHO CAN HELP?

AT DETAILED LEVEL, REVIEW EACH DESIRED
OUTCOME AND RESET THE ACTIONS FOR THE
FINAL 10 DAYS.

@90 DAYS CHECKLIST.

HAVE YOU ACHIEVED EVERYTHING YOU SET OUT TO ACHIEVE?	AT THE BEGINNING OF THE FIRST 100 DAYS, YOU HAD A SET OF CHALLENGES TO OVERCOME AND A SET OF DESIRED OUTCOMES TO BE ACHIEVED. HOW HAS YOUR RECORD OVER THE LAST 90 DAYS STACKED UP AGAINST THAT BACKDROP?
HAVE YOU LAID THE FOUNDATIONS FOR THE REST OF YOUR FIRST 12 MONTHS "IN OFFICE"?	REMEMBER, THE WHOLE POINT OF HAVING AN ACCELERATED START IS SO THAT YOU LAY THE RIGHT FOUNDATIONS FOR A SUCCESSFUL FIRST 12 MONTHS AND BEYOND? ARE YOU SATISFIED THAT YOU HAVE ACHIEVED THIS?
ARE YOUR STAKEHOLDERS SATISFIED WITH YOUR PERFORMANCE?	DO YOU KNOW WHAT PEOPLE' S PERCEPTIONS ARE – YOUR BOSS, YOUR PEERS, YOUR TEAM AND ANY OTHER RELEVANT (EG. YOUR CUSTOMERS)?
DO YOUR TEAM RESPECT YOU?	IT IS FASTER AND EASIER TO GET YOUR TEAM TO WORK HARDER IF THEY LIKE AND – MORE IMPORTANTLY – RESPECT YOU.

CHAPTER 05: @90 – 100 DAYS

HAS THE MARKET HEARD FROM YOU?	WAS THERE A FORMAL ROLE ANNOUNCEMENT TO THE MARKETPLACE TO SIGNAL THE IMPORTANCE OF THE ROLE AND THAT YOU ARE THE NEW PERSON IN CHARGE. MORE IMPORTANTLY, HAVE YOU DELIVERED A WIN INTO THE MARKETPLACE THAT BENEFITS YOUR CUSTOMERS?
CAN YOU LIST OUT YOUR (QUALITATIVE, AS WELL AS QUANTITATIVE) QUICK WINS?	WHAT HAVE BEEN THE KEY WINS SINCE THE BEGINNING OF YOUR FIRST 100 DAYS? THIS COULD BE ANYTHING FROM THE RECRUITMENT OF A KEY STRATEGIC HIRE TO EARLY DELIVERY OF $ RESULTS TO IMPROVED % CUSTOMER RETENTION ETC. EVERY SUCCESS IS IMPORTANT AND IT CAN BE VERY REASSURING TO LIST THEM AT THIS STAGE.
HOW WOULD YOU RATE YOUR OWN PERFORMANCE?	BE HONEST WITH YOURSELF. IN THE END, ONLY YOU CAN REALLY RATE THE EFFORT YOU HAVE PUT IN TO THIS NEW ROLE.

HOW WOULD YOUR BOSS RATE YOUR PERFORMANCE?	WHAT SIGNALS – POSITIVE OR OTHERWISE – IS YOUR BOSS SENDING OUT, IN TERMS OF HOW THEY RATE YOUR PERFORMANCE? HOW SUPPORTIVE ARE THEY IN TERMS OF ENSURING YOUR SUCCESS? DO YOU NEED TO MAKE ANY FINAL ASKS ON THEIR TIME AND SUPPORT, AS YOU WRAP UP YOUR FIRST 100 DAYS?
WHAT HAVE YOU LEARNED FROM THE WHOLE EXPERIENCE?	WHAT HAVE YOU LEARNED ABOUT YOURSELF, YOUR ROLE, YOUR ORGANISATION, YOUR MARKET? WHAT DO YOU KNOW NOW, THAT YOU DIDN'T KNOW AT THE BEGINNING OF THE FIRST 100 DAYS?
ARE YOU HAVING FUN?	ALL WORK AND NO FUN MAKE FOR AN OVERLY SERIOUS APPROACH TO WORK AND LIFE AND NOBODY WANTS TO WORK WITH SOMEONE TOO SERIOUS/TOO DULL(!).

CHAPTER 05: @90 – 100 DAYS
CONDUCT 450 DEGREE FEEDBACK

'IT IS BETTER TO KNOW'.

SOMEONE ONCE SAID, THE PROBLEM WITH FEEDBACK IS THAT NO ONE REALLY WANTS TO GIVE IT AND NO ONE REALLY WANTS TO RECEIVE IT! AT FIRST100™ WE ALWAYS SAY 'IT IS BETTER TO KNOW', IN THE CONTEXT OF FIRST 100 DAYS, IT IS BETTER TO KNOW SOONER RATHER THAN LATER IF THERE IS A LEADERSHIP STYLE ISSUE OR ANY UNWITTING CULTURAL GAFFES TAKING PLACE THAT ARE PREVENTING STAKEHOLDER RELATIONSHIP BUILDING AND LEADERSHIP PERFORMANCE ACCELERATION.

GATHER EARLY FEEDBACK AND CAPITALISE ON IT

Typically in the first 100 days, unless you go out of your way to gather information, feedback from your boss stays at surface level only (eg. 'you're doing a great job, just keep going').

My suggestion is that you hire an external third party to run your @90 days feedback exercise encompassing: upwards (your boss), at level (2-4 peers), below level (3-5 direct reports) and any other important role stakeholders (eg. customer).

This is a simple, effective and useful 360 exercise, but go even deeper to make it a 450 by also taking time out for self-reflection, to reduce blind-spots and unknowns.

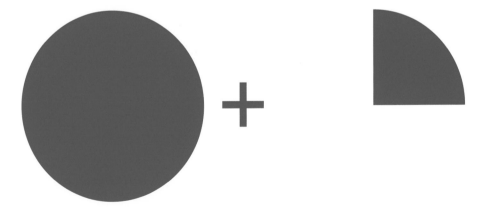

CHAPTER 05: @90 – 100 DAYS

@90 DAYS FIRST100ASSIST™
STAKEHOLDER FEEDBACK FORM.

SECTION 01: WHAT IS YOUR OVERALL IMPRESSION OF THE NEWLY APPOINTED
LEADER'S STYLE & IMPACT IN THE LAST 90-100 DAYS?

_____

_____

_____

_____

_____

_____

SECTION 02: LEADERSHIP SKILL.	PLEASE RANK THE LEADER'S PERFORMANCE AS HIGH, MEDIUM OR LOW. PLEASE PROVIDE COMMENTS AND EXAMPLES.
ON VISION STRATEGY – SETS A CLEAR DIRECTION.	
ON PEOPLE & TEAMS – BRINGS PEOPLE FORWARD.	
ON RESULTS & DELIVERABLES – GETS RIGHT RESULTS.	

SECTION 03: WHAT SUGGESTIONS/TIPS CAN YOU OFFER THE LEADER FOR MOVING FORWARD?

CONGRATULATIONS,

YOU HAVE SUCCESSFULLY COMPLETED YOUR FIRST 100 DAYS!

CHAPTER 06: CLOSE OUT

Consider the First 100 Days Plan to have been a javelin throw. At the time, you set out a number of outcomes to be achieved – then perhaps organisation life and market dynamics got in the way?

Not everybody completes everything that they set out to achieve in their plan. But let's hope you followed the instructions, and made it most of the way there. So now is the time to take stock, and record your achievements.

DID YOU ACHIEVE SOME/MOST/ALL OF YOUR DESIRED OUTCOMES BY THE END OF THE FIRST 100 DAYS?

WHAT ARE THE LESSONS LEARNED ABOUT: YOU, THE ROLE, THE ORGANISATION, THE MARKET?

CHAPTER 06: CLOSE OUT

I SUGGEST YOU USE THE FOLLOWING FIRST100ASSIST™ TEMPLATE
TO MAKE A FIRST 100 DAYS PRESENTATION TO YOUR BOSS/BOARD/
STAKEHOLDERS.

AT MACRO LEVEL.	MY ACHIEVEMENTS @100 DAYS.
ON VISION & STRATEGY	
ON PEOPLE & TEAMS	
ON RESULTS & DELIVERABLES	

AT MICRO LEVEL.	MY ACHIEVEMENTS @100 DAYS.
VERSUS MY 10 DESIRED OUTCOMES.	
LESSONS LEARNED:	
NEXT STEPS:	

CHAPTER 06: CLOSE OUT

In my experience, there are typically 2 key moments of judgement of the newly appointed executive:

— THE END OF THE FIRST 100 DAYS

— THE END OF THE FIRST 12 MONTHS.

SO, CLOSE OUT YOUR 100 DAY PLAN. MOVE FROM SHORT TERM IMPACT TO A LONGER TERM VIEW SUCH AS END OF YOUR FIRST 12 MONTHS OR THE END OF THE FINANCIAL YEAR, WHICHEVER MAKES MORE SENSE IN YOUR CONTEXT.

CONVERT YOUR LESSONS LEARNED, NEW KNOWLEDGE AND EXPERIENCE GAINED, INTO A SET OF PRIORITIES AND PLAN THAT TAKES YOU TO THE END OF THE FIRST YEAR.

CELEBRATE THE MOMENT, AND MOVE FORWARD

ORIGINS OF "THE FIRST 100 DAYS"

ORIGINS OF THE FIRST 100 DAYS
ORIGINS OF 'FIRST 100 DAYS' CONCEPT

Franklin D. Roosevelt's (FDR) inauguration as President of America on 4th March 1933 occurred in the middle of a terrifying bank panic. Historian Arthur Schlesinger described the mood at FDR's inauguration: "It was now a matter of seeing whether a representative democracy could conquer economic collapse. It was a matter of staving off violence - even, some thought - revolution."

Nearly 13 million people in the US - one in four - were jobless. Nineteen million people depended upon meagre relief payments to survive. Workers lucky enough to have jobs earned, on average, only two-thirds what they made at the start of the Depression in 1929. Many of those who had money lost it: four thousand banks collapsed in the first two months of 1933. So great was the emergency, some urged dictatorial powers, but FDR rejected the suspension of constitutional government. Instead he embarked on a plan to meet this vast crisis. The speed and scope of FDR's actions were unprecedented.

FDR's legendary "First 100 Days" concentrated on the first part of his strategy: immediate relief. He successfully prevented a run on the banks by immediately declaring a "bank holiday," closing all banks indefinitely until bankers and government could regain control of the situation. From March 9 to June 16, 1933, FDR sent Congress a record number of bills, all of which passed easily. The second part of his strategy was to provide long-lasting reform to the nation's economy.

Many later presidents have used the "First 100 Days" as a measure against which to mobilize their own administrations.

IN LESS THAN FOUR MONTHS THE AMERICAN ECONOMY WAS STABILIZED, HOMES AND FARMS WERE SAVED FROM FORECLOSURE, AND MASSIVE RELIEF AND WORK PROGRAMS ADDRESSED THE DIRE NEEDS OF THE PEOPLE.

MOST IMPORTANT, THE FIRST 100 DAYS RESTORED HOPE AND, IN THE PROCESS, PRESERVED DEMOCRATIC GOVERNMENT IN THE UNITED STATES.

ORIGINS OF THE FIRST 100 DAYS

See any interesting parallels between FDR and the challenges that faced President Barack Obama in his first 100 days in office? Faced with considerable pressure to get the American economy and the global economy back on track, it was worth noting that one of his first actions as President Elect was to announce his Two Year Plan –hitting the ground running so fast that even though there can only be one American president at a time, he had to demonstrate a fast start months ahead of official day one.

YOUR FIRST 100 DAYS CONTEXT WILL NOT BE AS DRAMATIC AS THAT OF FDR OR PRESIDENT BARACK OBAMA.

NONETHELESS, LEADERS IN TODAY'S HIGH PERFORMANCE CORPORATE ORGANISATIONS DO FIND THEMSELVES IN EXTREMELY PRESSURISED SITUATIONS AND NEED TO BE ABLE TO STEP UP WITH SPEED.

HIT THE GROUND RUNNING.